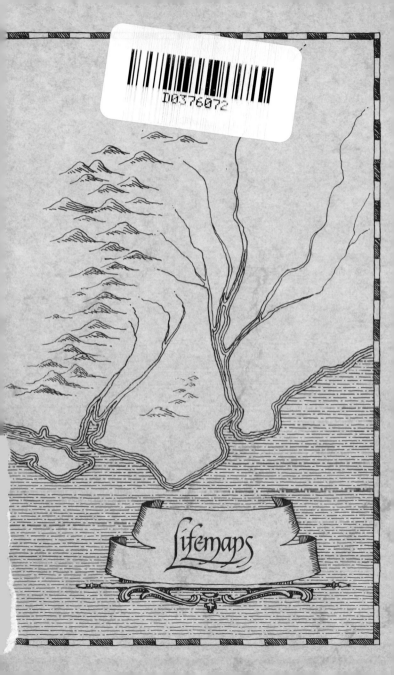

D0376072

Lifemaps

Leadership

Leadership

Influence That Inspires

Lifemaps™

WORD BOOKS
PUBLISHER
WACO, TEXAS

A DIVISION OF
WORD, INCORPORATED

LEADERSHIP: INFLUENCE THAT INSPIRES

Man of Steel and Velvet is from an address by Carl Sandburg given before the Eighty-sixth Congress, first session, 12 February 1959, Vol. 105, pp. 2265–2266.

Library of Congress Cataloging in Publication Data

Swindoll, Charles R.
  Leadership: influence that inspires.

  (Lifemaps)
  1. Christian leadership—Biblical teaching.
2. Bible.
N.T. Epistles of Paul—Criticism, interpretation, etc.
I. Title. II. Series.
BS2655.L42S9 1985   248.4   84-27104
ISBN 0-8499-0444-7

Printed in the United States of America

INTRODUCTION

Leadership is not optional; it is essential. Essential for motivation and direction. Essential for evaluation and accomplishment. It is the one ingredient essential for the success of any organization. Take away leadership and it isn't long before confusion replaces vision. Volunteers or employees who once dedicated themselves to their tasks begin to drift without leadership. Morale erodes. Enthusiasm fades. The whole system finally grinds to a halt.

Peter Drucker's famous line is both timeless and true: "If an enterprise fails to perform, we rightly hire, not different workers, but a new president." [1] When there's trouble brewing at the bottom, chances are good that a major part of the problem is at the top. Whether the scene is business, industry, labor, government, education, athletics, military, religion, or domestic, the hope and progress of the organization rests in the hands of those who are in charge.

Realizing the essential nature of leadership and having had numerous opportunities to witness both positive and negative examples of it, I recently found myself surprised to find so little written on the subject . . . from a *biblical* point of view. Oh, there are countless volumes on motivation and time management. There are many how-to-do-it books that address self-esteem and reaching one's full potential, but I find very few books on today's shelves that take the reader to the Scripture and allow God's Word to speak authoritatively on the subject of leadership. As you will see, the Bible has a great deal to say about leadership, and its counsel is both reliable and practical.

Because I am engaged in the Christian ministry as the pastor of a local church with a multiple staff, as well as being the president of an international radio ministry with more than one hundred employees, my world, as it relates to leadership, is anything but theoretical. The insights I share are being hammered out on the anvil of hands-on involvement with many people. While the major part of my work is in the religious realm, it is certainly not limited to that. Therefore, I can assure you that the ideas and principles I present are neither exclusive to the Christian who is in ministry nor are they in any sense of the word idealistic and/or irrelevant. If you are engaged in the business world or practicing a profession that calls for management skills, I can heartily recommend these pages to you just as unhesitatingly as I would urge a pastor or any other vocational Christian worker to read and heed my remarks.

While digging my way through one of the letters in the New Testament some time ago, I happened upon a section of Scripture that spoke with remarkable relevance on the subject of leadership. After speaking from the passage on several occasions, I invariably found myself surrounded by a cross-section of men and women of various ages and stages in life urging me to put these thoughts into print. Because these people represented the secular marketplace, both professionals as well as management and labor, plus a number of different Christian ministries at home and abroad, I began to take their urging seriously. The result is the book you hold in your hands. I hope you own a copy of the Scripture, because you need to hold that in your other hand. Apart from that Book, this book would have never come to pass.

If something I write triggers a new

idea or opens a door of hope, prompting fresh excitement or motivation that results in your becoming a better leader, I will be pleased. But I am really unable to take any of the credit. All I have done is go back to an infallible source that has never failed to give sound advice. That's why I decided over twenty-five years ago to dedicate myself to a lifetime study of the Scriptures. What leadership is to an organization, the Bible is to me—it isn't optional; it's essential.

Chuck Swindoll
Fullerton, California

Leadership is not optional;
it is essential

THE VALUE OF LEADERSHIP

During the prosperous sixties, Dunn and Bradstreet reported an average of more than thirteen thousand business failures annually. Natural and professional curiosity led them to search out why. Their analysis revealed that the lion's share of these casualties (approximately 92 percent) were due to managerial deficiencies. The facts don't lie—businesses don't fail until the leaders do.

Who hasn't gone into a restaurant that was once noted for its splendid reputation only to be disappointed? Instead of an elegant, enjoyable setting, the place looked run down, disappointingly unkempt. You expected superb service and delectable food placed before you in a creative and first-class manner, but both server and cuisine were a letdown. As an astute observer, you realized the problem wasn't simply an irresponsible maintenance crew or a preoccupied waiter or an amateur cook . . . it was management.

Who hasn't watched a favorite professional football team tumble from the top of the league to the bottom? Once a powerhouse of strength, innovation, and top-caliber players, the team now embarrasses its fans as one losing season follows another. The primary need is not another split end or a better linebacker or a bigger nose guard. Owners and team alike will agree that they need another coach. In some cases, another owner!

When Chrysler Corporation decided to get serious about solving its decline in the American automobile industry, it did not change the body style on its new cars or ask its dealers across the country to paint their buildings another color. No, Chrysler hired a new and innovative leader—Lee Iacocca. And now his name is fast becoming as famous as that of his former boss, Henry Ford. Not surprising to anyone, more and more people are buying Chrysler products.

During my years in the Marine Corps I watched the morale of the troops reversed within a brief span of time once a new battalion leader or company commander took charge. I have seen churches, once devastated by splits or scandals, turn the corner and reach new heights in their ministry as the right leadership was chosen and given the reins of responsibility. I have also witnessed towns and cities shake off reputations for being crime-ridden and dangerous places to live or for being dirty and lacking self-respect—once they put into office civic leaders with a high degree of integrity, determination, and courage. And how could one deny the value of leadership within a home? Parents or guardians who are loving, affirming, fair, and consistent in their discipline, and secure and confident in their relationship with their children—my, what a difference in that family!

LEADERSHIP DEFINED

But wait. I have mentioned a lot of things about the value of leadership, about its essential nature in a business, a church, a team, a home. But I haven't defined it. Actually, it is difficult to define. It's much easier to describe what leaders do than to describe what they are. Good leadership is, more often than not, elusive. We know it when we see it, yet we have a tough time identifying and capsulizing the concept.

At the risk of oversimplifying, I'm going to resist a long, drawn-out definition and settle on one word. It's the word *influence*. If you will allow me two words—*inspiring influence.*

Those who do the best job of management—those most successful as leaders—use their influence to inspire others to follow, to work harder, to sacrifice, if necessary. Elusive though it may be, such inspiring influence generates incredible results. When a team finds leadership in the coach, it is remarkable how the players will strive for and achieve almost impossible feats to win. When a teacher has leadership abilities, the cooperation and accomplishments of the class border on the astounding. When a sales force finds leadership in their manager, they will knock themselves out to reach their quotas month in, month out.

This is a good time to clarify something, lest you get the false impression that all leaders must have the same temperament. Not so. Some are hard-charging types whose style is bold, loud, and strong. But others, equally effective, may be much quieter. They seldom lift their voices above a conversational level. I know leaders who employ extrinsic methods of motivation with a great degree of success. But I'm also acquainted with those who loathe that approach. They would much rather motivate the inner person with intrinsic appeals. Then there are leaders who remain aloof while others roll up their sleeves and get personally involved with those they lead. Some leaders are highly intelligent, widely read, and scholarly in their approach. Others are not as bright intellectually, but they are seasoned, wise, and resourceful—yet just as respected as their brilliant counterparts.

Obviously, a leader's temperament (some may prefer to call it "style") will differ from one personality to the next. However leadership style may come across, those who respond with cooperation and commitment do so because of the inspiring influence that leader emits.

For the sake of further clarification, I

should also mention that regardless of temperament, the leader whose influence proves most effective is the one who gets along well with people. The great American entrepreneur, John D. Rockefeller, once admitted, "I will pay more for the ability to deal with people than any other ability under the sun." [2] The value of this single quality can hardly be exaggerated. According to a report by the American Management Association, an overwhelming majority of the two hundred managers who participated in the survey agreed that the single most valuable ingredient—the "paramount skill"—was the ability to get along with people. Managers rated this ability above intelligence, decisiveness, job knowledge, or technical skills.[3]

Before moving on to an outstanding biblical example, I want to add a comment to those who are in vocational Christian service. All too often (especially among those getting started in ministry) the importance of getting along well with people is played down. It is erroneously assumed that people will automatically respect and follow one's leadership simply because of a mutual commitment to the same Lord or a mutual agreement to the same doctrine—regardless of the leader's ability to deal with people. That is a most unhappy delusion! Time and again I have spoken with disillusioned individuals who began their service for the King with that mentality. Although they were called, schooled, dedicated, excited about their future, and faced with a choice opportunity to lead a group of people, they ultimately found themselves forced to face the fact that the one ingredient they thought could be overlooked was the very one they could not do without. How often I have heard the words, "If only . . . ." More about that later.

So then, let's expand our definition to include these all-important characteristics. Effective leaders are those whose inspiring influence prompts others to follow. While their style, level of intelligence, methods of motivation, and personal involvement with the tasks may differ widely, those people who are most successful possess the same trait—the ability to get along well with others.

A BIBLICAL MODEL

Background

The New Testament letter I referred to in my introduction is the first letter written by a first-century missionary named Paul. It was sent to a small but capable band of Christians living in the bustling, wealthy metropolis of Thessalonica. Today, it's the Grecian city of Thessalonike (or Salonika), second only to Athens in size. Like many in our busy American cities, the Thessalonians were living in the fast lane (an ancient freeway—named *Via Ignatia*—ran alongside the city) and were active citizens of a colorful and aggressive culture. Merchants, businessmen and career women, artists and laborers, philosophers and teachers comprised that small Christian community. Many of them could remember the day when they first heard the Jewish traveler from Tarsus as he spoke so courageously, so convincingly, of his conversion and of their need to believe in the Lord Jesus Christ. How could they resist?

As a sufficient number of them responded, the little church in Macedonia (northern Greece) was born and after a few short weeks, almost as quickly as he had arrived, Paul departed. His entire stay was not longer than two months, probably less. His travels took him on through Athens to Corinth, from where he wrote this first letter to his friends in Thessalonica. About a year had passed. Who knows what precise thought prompted Paul to pick up his pen and begin to write? Concern? Curiosity? Nostalgia? Some traveler's comment who spoke to him one night in Corinth?

Perhaps a mixture of all the above. The missionary began to muse. He retraced his steps and relived the excitement of those weeks he had invested in Macedonia. What eventful days! What a great group of believers!

Initial Feelings

Just imagine the man's emotions as he wrote:

> For you yourselves know, brethren, that our coming to you was not in vain, but after we had already suffered and been mistreated in Philippi, as you know, we had the boldness in our God to speak to you the gospel of God amid much opposition (1 Thess. 2:1–2).

How many of us would love to look back over our shoulder someday and say, "Now *that* was not in vain!" All those hours and days and months that Paul had invested among the Thessalonians were purposeful . . . not empty, not hollow. Much was accomplished. It was worth all the effort. Lives were changed. Decisions that relate to eternity were made. "Not in vain!"

Then, almost as if he is struck with a glimpse of grief, Paul adds a comment about the pain he endured prior to his arrival. He mentions how fractured he felt when he stumbled into their city. Philippi, his previous place of ministry, had been no friend of grace to help him on to God. There had been shameful mistreatment. "Outrageous" would say it better and be more in keeping with Paul's actual choice of terms. While in that city he and his companion Silas had been beaten with rods and dumped into prison. We Christians love to talk about how miraculously they were later delivered from that awful place. But we seldom linger over the humiliation—the inhuman treatment—they endured prior to their glorious deliverance. Although torn in body, the missionary did not hesitate to speak boldly of the good news of Messiah immediately upon arriving at Thessalonica. But even that was "amid much opposition," please remember.

What's the point of all this, you may wonder. I thought we were dealing with effective leadership, not a story about pain and suffering. We are doing all three; they are usually inseparable.

Far too many today live in a dream world when it comes to preparation for leadership. There is this popular yet mistaken notion that leaders somehow emerge on the scene having been dropped from a lacy cloud—all white, ideal, and spotless—like a living Mr. Clean, "untouched by human hands." Perhaps that is the reason God led Paul to go back to those painful days when many would have said, "Now, that *was* in vain!" But it wasn't. What a perfect place to begin when building a biblical model of leadership . . . the pain of mistreatment, the humiliation and loneliness of being imprisoned.

Some (dare I say *most?*) of God's

choicest leaders have emerged from wombs of woe. The ghetto. A prison. Shame or sickness. A broken home. Mistreatment and fear. But resiliently and triumphantly they came through. From a stormy and tumultuous world of outward opposition or personal insecurity or emotional breakdown or financial failure or physical affliction, they stand today as living trophies of grace.

My point? Disabilities need not disqualify. On the contrary, struggling makes a great background for leadership! Not unless you have struggled with the hopelessness and brokenness of life's pains can you possibly know how to lead others through such valleys. Since the prime function of the leader is to keep hope alive, having been bereft of it helps the leader never to forget the value of it. Yesterday's pain prompts today's praise.

It was just such thoughts that caused Aleksandr Solzhenitsyn to write:

It was only when I lay there on rotting prison straw that I sensed within myself the first stirrings of good. Gradually, it was disclosed to me that the line separating good and evil passes, not through states, nor between classes, nor between political parties either, but right through every human heart, and through all human hearts. So, bless you, prison, for having been in my life.[4]

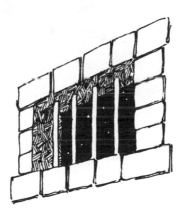

WHAT TO OMIT FOR EFFECTIVE LEADERSHIP

Once Paul began to reflect upon his not-in-vain visit among the Thessalonians, he opened a floodgate of memories. Living almost twenty centuries removed from those days, we have difficulty imagining how the man could have continued on in spite of the difficulties he encountered. Furthermore, what characterized his leadership? How could he have been so bold? When the Thessalonians remembered him in their midst, what mental images did they entertain? All these questions and so many more are answered in the section following these opening lines we have just been reliving.

He mentions several things that did *not* characterize his leadership before presenting the things that did. Let's observe the negatives before considering the positives. There are four of each.

Deception

> For our exhortation does not come from error or impurity or by way of deceit (1 Thess. 2:3).

The self-portrait Paul paints is one of absolute honesty and sincerity. Not double-tongued, guilty of a hidden agenda or improper motives, he admits to being free from deception.

Great place to start! And all the more important since the leader has clout. There is a built-in role of authority just by virtue of the position he or she holds. Except for a few who view any and all leaders with a critical eye, most folks

trust and hold their leader in high regard
. . . making leaders easy, unsuspecting
targets of deception by those who lack
integrity.

Decades ago Elton Trueblood wrote
like a prophet far ahead of his time:

> It is hard to think of any job in which
> the moral element is lacking. The skill of
> the dentist is wholly irrelevant if he is
> unprincipled and irresponsible. There is
> little, in that case, to keep him from
> extracting teeth unnecessarily, because
> the patient is usually in a helpless situation.
> It is easy to see the harm that can be done
> by an unprincipled lawyer. Indeed, such
> a man is far more dangerous if he is skilled
> than if he is not skilled.[5]

I frequently quote to myself the
statement made by Asaph, who wrote
eloquently of David the king. After his
masterful treatise on the early history of
the Hebrew people in Psalm 78, he
reserved the final three verses for David,
almost like a climactic benediction.

He also chose David His servant,
And took him from the sheepfolds;
From the care of the ewes with suckling
    lambs He brought him,
To shepherd Jacob His people,
And Israel His inheritance.
So he [David] shepherded them according
    to the integrity of his heart,
And he guided them with skillful hands.

Leaders with power and brains are common. So are leaders with riches and popularity. But a competent leader who has integrity and skill, coupled with sincerity, is rare indeed. Deception creates suspicion. Once the leader's followers begin to suspect motives or find that what is said publicly is denied privately, the thin wire of respect that holds everything in place snaps. Confidence is drained away. The late President Dwight Eisenhower stated his opinion with dogmatism:

> . . . the supreme quality for a leader is unquestionably integrity. Without it, no

real success is possible, no matter whether it is a section gang, on a football field, in an army, or in an office. If his associates find him guilty of phoniness, if they find that he lacks forthright integrity, he will fail. His teachings and actions must square with each other. The first great need, therefore, is integrity and high purpose.[6]

Flattery

> But just as we have been approved by God to be entrusted with the gospel, so we speak, not as pleasing men but God, who examines our hearts. For we never came with flattering speech, as you know . . . (1 Thess. 2:4–5a).

Of course, Paul made this statement referring to the gospel he preached. I believe it has a broader application as well in the realm of leadership. And it is especially difficult if you are good in working with people! There is a fine but very definite line between being a leader who gets along well with people and being one who must please people. Few characteristics reveal one's insecurity more than this. And talk about losing respect! Not only do others fail to respect the people-pleaser, he doesn't even respect himself. By fence-sitting, by hedging with the truth and attempting to keep peace at any price (an absolute impossibility), the leader forfeits the right to lead and becomes, as a consequence, a follower who still tries to call himself a leader.

This reminds me of something about which too little has been said. I can think of few ingredients more foundational to being a good leader than knowing oneself—and accepting oneself—and feeling secure about oneself inside one's own skin. The scene is nothing short of tragic when an insecure person is given a leadership responsibility. One of the earliest signs is the very point Paul makes—flattery is substituted for decisiveness.

Allow me this direct question: Do you

know yourself? And one more: Do you like yourself? Apart from these basic stones being in place, the superstructure of meaningful accomplishment becomes a study in futility. Let me urge you to start here, if you have hopes of being successful as a leader. It may take great effort to gain a secure sense of self-esteem, it may involve a painful process, but in the long haul you will be grateful you paid the price. Not until you have peace with yourself, not until you know and like the things that make you what you are, will you be able to conquer the need to flatter.

In her splendid work, *Gift from the Sea,* Anne Morrow Lindbergh states her credo. It drips with an abundance of personal security.

I want, first of all . . . to be at peace with myself. I want a singleness of eye, a purity of intention, a central core to my life that will enable me to carry out these obligations and activities as well as I can.

I want, in fact—to borrow from the language of the saints—to live "in grace" as much of the time as possible. I am not using this term in a strictly theological sense. By grace I mean an inner harmony, essentially spiritual, which can be translated into outward harmony. I am seeking perhaps what Socrates asked for in the prayer from the Phaedrus when he said, "May the outward and the inward man be one." I would like to achieve a state of inner spiritual grace from which I could function and give as I was meant to in the eye of God.[7]

Maybe it will help you to look back at that statement Paul made to the Thessalonians. We Christians have been "approved by God" and therefore He alone "examines our hearts." It seems to me that He holds much of the secret to overcoming this insecure tendency to be a people-pleaser. Before moving on, take a look at Galatians 1:10. There was a time in my ministry, many years ago, when this single verse of Scripture jolted me back to a place of confidence, delivering me from the trap of telling a group of influential people what they wanted to hear. I realize now it was a turning point in my leadership pilgrimage from slave to others to servant of Christ.

For am I now seeking the favor of men, or of God? Or am I striving to please men? If I were still trying to please men, I would not be a bondservant of Christ (Gal. 1:10).

Just as there is no place for deception in a leader who wants to be respected, neither can there be the habit of flattery. As some wag once said: "I don't know the secret of success, but I do know the secret of failure—try to please everybody!" No successful leader maintains the respect of others without making decisions that will prove unpopular to some.

Greed

> For we never came with flattering
> speech, as you know, nor with a pretext
> for greed—God is witness—(1 Thess. 2:5).

Interestingly, Paul tells his readers
that they themselves could testify to the
fact that he did not speak with flattering
speech ("as you know"). However, when
it came to his refusing to conduct his
life according to greed, "God is witness."
When the leader is a people-pleaser,
anyone can see that. It's no secret. It is
public knowledge. But greed can be
hidden, masked from public view. Yet
the One who examines hearts knows the
whole truth.

What a motivational cancer is greed!
It's not simply the longing to get more
. . . but the passion to possess more than
one ought to possess. Greed doesn't stop
with healthy and necessary competition;
it strives to have the most at any cost.
With wicked determination this ruthless
beast scratches and claws its way to the

top, snarling defiantly and devouring whatever and whomever gets in its way.

Earlier in this book I mentioned the appointment of a dynamic new leader at Chrysler, the former president of Ford Motor Company, Lee Iacocca. While reading the autobiography of this hard-boiled entrepreneur, I was interested to discover his feelings about greed. After being fired by Ford, Iacocca was forced to rethink his motives and answer some gut-level questions regarding his reasons for hanging on so tenaciously to his job at Ford. His confession of greed is not hidden. Face it, it's tough for anyone to turn his back on almost a million a year, plus perks! A guy who has white-coated waiters available at the snap of his fingers and a chauffeur to and from work finds it extremely difficult to put on the brakes. In a moment of vulnerable honesty, the man admits that of the seven deadly sins, greed is by far the worst. Hear him as he quotes his Italian-born father:

My father always said, "Be careful about money. When you have five thousand, you'll want ten. And when you have ten, you'll want twenty." He was right. No matter what you have, it's never enough.[8]

The path of many a leader is strewn with the litter of greed. Like the remora, those little shark suckers that swim alongside and attach themselves to the great sharks of the sea, greed is always near those in leadership . . . and the more influential the leader, the more the temptation to yield. And do not be so foolish as to think it's limited to those in the marketplace. Greed is just as aggressive in the Christian ministry! Greed for larger crowds, more impressive results, bigger buildings, even greed for fame among one's own circles.

Greed has three facets: love of things, love of fame, and love of pleasure; and these can be attacked directly with frugality, anonymity, and moderation.

Reduction of greed will be translated into stepped-up vitality, diminished self-centeredness, and a clearer awareness of our real identity. For a permanent commitment to working with the tools of the spiritual life provides a disciplined basis for liberation from greed's tentacles.[9]

Not a bad set of priorities to pursue, especially if the desire for more, more, more is beginning to take its toll.

Authoritarianism

For we never came with flattering speech, as you know, nor with a pretext for greed—God is witness—nor did we seek glory from men, either from you or from others, even though as apostles of Christ we might have asserted our authority (1 Thess. 2:5–6).

Not having lived in the first century, we have difficulty appreciating Paul's comment regarding his role as an "apostle of Christ." There was no higher title in the church, no more powerful or influential position than apostleship. Wherever he went, whatever he did, whenever he spoke authentic apostolic authority accompanied it. Paul was the E. F. Hutton of the early church—people stopped everything and listened! But this apostle was different from what you might expect. Instead of massaging his image and playing the role of the Caesar of the church, he restrained himself. He refused to assert his authority . . . even though (as he admits) he had every right to do so. When others attempted to glorify him, he rejected it. When special treatment was offered, Paul turned it down. As a matter of fact, in his next letter to them we read that he carried his share of the financial responsibilities, lest he appear as a freeloader.

> For you yourselves know how you ought to follow our example, because we did not act in an undisciplined manner among you, nor did we eat anyone's bread without paying for it, but with labor and

hardship we kept working night and day so that we might not be a burden to any of you; not because we do not have the right to this, but in order to offer ourselves as a model for you, that you might follow our example. For even when we were with you, we used to give you this order; if anyone will not work, neither let him eat (2 Thess. 3:7–10).

Leaders—especially those with vast influence—frequently fall into the trap of throwing their weight around and expecting kid-glove treatment. How unusual yet how encouraging to find true humility and a servant's heart among those who have a lot of clout! Too many use their leadership status to lord it over, to take advantage of those they lead, thinking their prima-donna style comes with the territory they now possess. People become little more than pawns on a chessboard of gamelike moves, where authoritarian leaders play out their goals and objectives.

Michael Macoby of Harvard University, author of *The Gamesmen,* vividly portrays this person as:

> . . . the leader who plays games with ideas and objectives, resources, and with people . . . he plays at leadership; he gets his "kicks" out of making things work. His main concern: that he is successful . . . as long as he can hang one more trophy over the fireplace of recognition, as long as he is properly remunerated. [10]

Picking up on this whole idea, Gordon MacDonald, minister-at-large of World Vision, adds this insightful, albeit penetrating reminder:

> The gamesman is not an alien within the Christian community. One can see traces of gamesmanship entangling itself in vast areas of Christian activity. It is an insidious influence that leads Christians to measure the work of God in terms of numbers, square footage, and popular acceptance . . . .

Today the theme that overrides any other is that of *me first* in blessing; *me first* in the feel-good experience of certain spiritual gifts; *me first* in terms of material comfort and rewards . . . . The bottom line of the contemporary gospel—the one that does not produce servants—seems to be "grab the crown; avoid the cross!" [11]

So then, these four things are to be omitted if you wish to have a philosophy of leadership that squares with Scripture:

- Deception
- Flattery
- Greed
- Authoritarianism

WHAT TO INCLUDE FOR
EFFECTIVE LEADERSHIP

So much for the negatives. Now let's
concentrate on the positive traits, of
which there are also four. By reading
through the next section of this letter,
each one emerges.

Sensitivity to Needs

But we proved to be gentle among you,
as a nursing *mother* tenderly cares for her
own children (1 Thess. 2:7).

Still reflecting on his days among
them, which were "not in vain," Paul

gets a bit misty. He compares himself to a nursing mother who graciously and unselfishly cares for the needs of her own children. Without hesitation he uses terms like gentleness and tenderness to describe his approach—words seldom associated with competent leaders who get the job done.

But this brings me back to an earlier remark I made regarding getting along well with others. Leaders who do the best job are those whose antennae are keenly attuned to others. They sense the scene, they get the picture, they read between the lines. And having done so, they operate from that sensitive vantage point, which weaves wisdom and understanding into the fabric of their leadership. Those who respond to such leaders do so with delight because they realize their leader cares . . . cares about them personally; they don't just check folks off like items on the agenda. To carry this out, the leader must guard against a major enemy—preoccupation.

He must force himself to do more than see, he must have *insight*. He must do more than hear, he must *perceive*. The most effective leaders have the uncanny ability to spot what isn't said, to detect attitudes behind actions, facial expressions surrounding words being spoken.

I laughed out loud when I read psychologist James Dobson's account of a physician whose preoccupation reached the maximum extreme. With tongue in cheek, Dr. Dobson writes:

> I know of a gynecologist who is not only deaf, but blind as well. He telephoned a friend of mine who is also a physician in the practice of obstetrics and gynecology. He asked for a favor.
>
> "My wife has been having some abdominal problems and she's in particular discomfort this afternoon," he said. "I don't want to treat my own wife and wonder if you'd see her for me?"
>
> My friend invited the doctor to bring his wife for an examination, whereupon

he discovered (are you ready for this?) that she was five months pregnant! Her obstetrician husband was so busy caring for other patients that he hadn't even noticed his wife's burgeoning pregnancy. I must admit wondering how in the world this woman ever got his attention long enough to conceive! [12]

Affection for People

Having thus a fond affection for you, we were well-pleased to impart to you not only the gospel of God but also our own lives, because you had become very dear to us (1 Thess. 2:8).

Once again we are somewhat surprised to read of such things as love and a warm, affectionate relationship being important ingredients in effective leadership. But indeed they are! Even to one as disciplined and determined as Paul, feelings of "fond affection" were considered invaluable. Why? Because those he led became "very dear" to him.

Even though Paul was tough enough to do pioneer work and brilliant enough to hammer out his theology on a realistic anvil of physical abuse and emotional trauma, his genuine affection for people came through loud and clear. Whether young or old, famous or obscure, healthy or sickly, sharp or dull, people who got close to the great apostle of grace felt loved because they *were* loved.

Because this relates so closely with the next positive characteristic, I want to mention it in conjunction with affection for people.

Authenticity of Life

Nor did we eat anyone's bread without paying for it, but with labor and hardship we kept working night and day so that we might not be a burden to any of you; not because we do not have the right to this, but in order to offer ourselves as a model for you, that you might follow our example (1 Thess. 2:9–10).

I tie these together for a definite reason. A leader who has affection for people must somehow *demonstrate* that affection. This requires authenticity and even a measure of transparency. Did you catch what Paul said about his personal style? I don't want us to miss it, since it's a major secret of good leadership. He was pleased to impart, "not only the gospel," but also his "own life." With that kind of leader, you didn't have to settle for a truckload of truth dumped into your ears and nothing more. You also got, along with the truth, authentic reality—his own life. He had nothing to hide.

Paul goes on to say he worked among them, and in doing so, he behaved "uprightly and blamelessly." In other words he practiced what he preached. Is it any wonder God was pleased to use this leader to such a remarkable extent? No pompous air about him. No distant, demanding despot who came, saw, and conquered. No visiting lecturer who remained aloof and lived in a world of touch-me-not secrecy. On the contrary, he was approachable, accessible, a leader who loved, whom people could get next to, whom God would use to shape the early history of His church.

It was not unusual for Paul to be this open. Time and again in his letters, he combined authenticity with affection.

For example, consider similar words to the Corinthians.

And when I came to you, brethren, I did not come with superiority of speech or of wisdom, proclaiming to you the testimony of God. For I determined to know nothing among you except Jesus Christ, and Him crucified. And I was with you in weakness and in fear and in much trembling, and my message and my preaching were not in persuasive words of wisdom, but in demonstration of the Spirit and of power, that your faith should not rest on the wisdom of men, but on the power of God (1 Cor. 2:1–5).

He wrote just as openly of his trials and struggles. None of that was considered his own secret world. While he did not play on others' emotions to manipulate them, he remained vulnerable and unguarded when it came to his own humanity . . . as when he wrote his friends in Philippi:

It has been a great joy to me that after all this time you have shown such interest in my welfare. I don't mean that you had forgotten me, but up till now you had no opportunity of expressing your concern. Nor do I mean that I have been in actual need for I have learned to be content, whatever the circumstances may be. I know now how to live when things are difficult and I know how to live when things are prosperous. In general and in particular I have learned the secret of facing either poverty or plenty. I am ready for anything through the strength of the one who lives within me. Nevertheless I am not disparaging the way in which you were willing to share my troubles. You

Philippians will remember that in the early days of the Gospel when I left Macedonia, you were the only Church who shared with me the fellowship of giving and receiving. Even in Thessalonica you twice sent me help when I was in need. It isn't the value of the gift that I am keen on; it is the reward that will come to you because of these gifts that you have made.

Now I have everything I want—in fact I am rich. Yes, I am quite content, thanks to your gifts received through Epaphroditus. Your generosity is like a lovely fragrance, a sacrifice that pleases the very heart of God.[13]

The popular yet mistaken mental image of a successful leader is the tough-minded executive who is always in control, who holds himself aloof, who operates in a world of untouchable, sophisticated secrecy. If he or she has needs, feels alone, wrestles with very human problems, lacks the ability to cope with some particular pressure . . .

no one should ever know about it. And *certainly* there is no place for tears! That would be a sign of weakness, and real leaders don't cry . . . nor do they evidence any other emotion than a self-assured air of confidence.

Where did we pick up such inhuman ideas? Since when is it a sign of weakness to be real—to admit needs—to show affection? Why do we have such an aversion for tears? The best leaders, the men and women in my life who have impacted me most significantly, have usually been those who allowed me entrance into their private world, who expressed (and proved) their love for me. Often when they hurt, they wept. When they were unsure, they said so. When they struggled, they admitted it. They were strong and competent, but nevertheless 100 percent human and real. The combination only deepened my respect.

On the one-hundred-fiftieth anniversary of the birthday of Abraham

Lincoln, the distinguished poet and historian Carl Sandburg was invited to Washington D.C. to speak. Before a joint session of Congress and assembled diplomatic corps, the astute, eloquent student of Lincoln held the attention of everyone as he portrayed a very great leader with very human characteristics. Calling his speech, appropriately, *Man of Steel and Velvet,* Sandburg helped everyone see that a respected leader can be both capable and vulnerable. The mixture may be rare, but when it is there it is truly effective.

Not often in the story of mankind does a man arrive on earth who is both steel and velvet, who is as hard as rock and soft as drifting fog, who holds in his heart and mind the paradox of terrible storm and peace unspeakable and perfect . . . .

While the war winds howled, he insisted that the Mississippi was one river meant to belong to one country . . . .

While the luck of war wavered and broke and came again, as generals failed and campaigns were lost, he held enough forces . . . together to raise new armies and supply them, until generals were found who made war as victorious war has always been made, with terror, frightfulness, destruction . . . valor and sacrifice past words of man to tell.

In the mixed shame and blame of the immense wrongs of two crashing civilizations, often with nothing to say, he said nothing, slept not at all, and on occasions he was seen to weep in a way that made weeping appropriate, decent, majestic.

Enthusiastic in Affirmation

You are witnesses, and so is God, how devoutly and uprightly and blamelessly we behaved toward you believers; just as you know how we were exhorting and encouraging and imploring each one of you as a father would his own children, so that you may walk in a manner worthy of the God who calls you into His own kingdom and glory (1 Thess. 2:10–12).

Did you notice those descriptive terms? "Exhorting . . . encouraging . . . imploring." And did you catch the analogy? ". . . as a father would His own children." Earlier Paul wrote of the tenderness of a nursing mother. Here he mentions the enthusiastic affirmation of a father.

It is not a picture of oppressive and relentless harassment, but rather reassuring encouragement . . . the you-can-do-it, hang-in-there confidence of a dad with his children.

My wife and I have reared four children. Two are now married, two are teenagers still living at home. All four have been students at the same high school, which means we have attended more high school football games than we can count! Because both of our sons have played on the team and both of our daughters have been cheerleaders, our interest has been more than casual. Those exciting autumn nights, the ecstasy of a last-minute winning touchdown pass as well as the agony of a missed field goal . . . winning the championship as well as losing that final game, these are among our most cherished memories shared as a family.

During our years in the bleachers, we have sat in the rooting section and screamed ourselves hoarse on more than a few occasions. Surrounded by other parents with an equally dedicated interest in the game, we have often found ourselves completely caught up in the game. My all-time favorite place to sit is near the father of our team's quarterback. The father-son connection is something to behold. Now you understand that the boy on the field cannot actually hear his dad in the stands, but there is, nevertheless, this "running dialogue" as the father encourages his son under his breath to press on . . . to be tough . . . to get that ball down the field.

Sometimes it is uncanny how the dad (who has all the plays memorized) will call the next play and the son will do exactly as he is "told." I have laughed as the dad will mumble words of positive affirmation. Then the son picks himself up after being sacked and marches the team right down the field to victory. I have even turned around and congratulated the volunteer coach in the stands for his incredible game plan!

In all our years of attending high school football games, I have never once heard the father of a player stand up and shout, "Take my son outa there . . . he's doing a terrible job. Put him on the bench!" Of course not! Why? Because it is the most natural tendency of fathers to "exhort . . . encourage . . . implore." their sons. Good dads affirm, they never condemn and attack their children. They believe in them to the very end.

And so it is with good leaders. With enthusiastic and reassuring words of affirmation, they help others to continue to believe in themselves, to do their very best.

Can you remember the four positive characteristics of good leadership? Let me review them:

- Sensitivity to needs
- Affection for people
- Authenticity of life
- Enthusiastic in affirmation

CONCLUSION

With care and concern for God's counsel on leadership, we have gone to the most reliable Book to find the guidelines worth following. We have discovered ways to implement an inspiring influence on others that will result in a greater desire to cooperate and a deeper commitment to getting the job done.

If you are serious about wanting to have a lasting and beneficial impact in others' lives as a leader who is uniquely used of God, I suggest that you regularly review these eight points I have presented. Write them down on a card and put that card in a conspicuous place, perhaps on the visor of your car, under the glass at your desk, or on a mirror in your home. While going over the list, pray. Pray for the ability to carry out each of these objectives in the sphere of your particular situation. Ask for patience, for wisdom, for determination, and for the ability to remain calm. As your day unfolds maintain a three-dimensional perspective.

- *Look in.* Reflect on the value of being a person of strong inner security.
- *Look around.* Realize that a commitment to excellence requires tenacity of purpose.
- *Look up.* Remember that you are not alone . . . that the Lord of heaven is still in control.

This is a perfect opportunity for me to mention the importance of a strong faith. It is easy for determined leaders to omit the spiritual dimension while pursuing a successful career. Numerous other involvements will seem so much more important that you'll be tempted to put this one off until later. Because his life illustrates so vividly the world most leaders can identify with, I want to conclude this book with a significant slice out of another leader's life. His name is Howard Rutledge.

While an American Air Force pilot, Rutledge was shot down over North Viet Nam during the early part of that war. For several miserable years, before being released at the war's conclusion, Howard Rutledge endured mistreatment at the hands of brutal captors. Following his release he reflected upon those years when his life was reduced to torturous silence and intolerable loneliness.

During those longer periods of enforced reflection it became so much easier to separate the important from the trivial,

the worthwhile from the waste. For
example, in the past, I usually worked or
played hard on Sundays and had no time
for church. For years Phyllis [his wife] had
encouraged me to join the family at
church. She never nagged or scolded—she
just kept hoping. But I was too busy, too
preoccupied, to spend one or two short
hours a week thinking about the really
important things.

Now the sights and sounds and smells
of death were all around me. My hunger
for spiritual food soon outdid my hunger
for a steak. Now I wanted to know about
that part of me that will never die. Now
I wanted to talk about God and Christ and
the church. But in Heartbreak [the name
POW's gave their prison camp] solitary
confinement, there was no pastor, no
Sunday-School teacher, no Bible, no
hymnbook, no community of believers to
guide and sustain me. I had completely
neglected the spiritual dimension of my
life. It took prison to show me how empty
life is without God.[14]

You are not a prisoner of war. Chances
are good that your life is moving along

at a pretty fast clip, perhaps so fast you've not taken the time to "separate the worthwhile from the waste," as Rutledge puts it. You may also have "completely neglected the spiritual dimension" of your life—a common yet tragic occurrence among busy leaders-in-the-making.

If so, pause and reflect. Then, like a good leader, be decisive. Turn your life over to the only One who can bring order and peace. His name is Jesus. Take him now. Believe me, this decision is essential, not optional.

NOTES

1. Frank Goble, *The Men at the Top* (Thornwood, NY: Caroline House Publishers, 1972), p. 1.

2. Ted W. Engstrom, *The Making of a Christian Leader* (Grand Rapids, MI: Zondervan Publishing House, 1976), p. 67.

3. Ted W. Engstrom, p. 67.

4. Philip Yancey, *Where Is God When It Hurts?* (Grand Rapids, MI: Zondervan Publishing House, 1977), p. 51.

5. Gordon MacDonald, *Facing Turbulent Times* (Wheaton, IL: Tyndale House Publisher, Inc. 1981), p. 93.

6. Dwight Eisenhower, "Leadership" *Quote Unquote*, Lloyd Cory, ed. (Wheaton, IL: Victor Books, a division of SP Publications, Inc. 1977), p. 177.

7. Anne Morrow Lindbergh, *Gift from the Sea* (New York, NY: Pantheon Publisher, a division of Random House, 1955), pp. 23–24.

8. Lee Iacocca, *Iacocca: An Autobiography* (New York, NY: Bantam Books, 1984), p. 146.

9. Paul Martin, "Greed," *Quote Unquote*, Lloyd Cory, ed. (Wheaton, IL: Victor Books, a division of SP Publications, Inc., 1977), p. 141.

10. Gordon MacDonald, p. 103.

11. Gordon MacDonald, pp. 103, 104.

12. James C. Dobson, *Straight Talk to Men and Their Wives* (Waco, TX: Word Books Publisher, 1980), p. 96.

13. J. B. Phillips, ed., *The New Testament in Modern English* (New York, NY: The Macmillan Company, 1960), p. 427.

14. Howard Rutledge and Phyllis Rutledge with Mel White and Lyla White, *In the Presence of Mine Enemies* (Old Tappan, NJ: Fleming H. Revell, 1973), p. 34.